Published by Creative Education
and Creative Paperbacks
P.O. Box 227, Mankato, Minnesota 56002
Creative Education and Creative Paperbacks
are imprints of The Creative Company
www.thecreativecompany.us

Design by The Design Lab
Production by Travis Green
Art direction by Rita Marshall
Printed in the United States of America

Photographs by Corbis (James Hager/Robert Hard-
ing World Imagery, Jami Tarris), Dreamstime (Crazy-
80frog, Isselee, Lovingyou2911, Pavlos Rekas, Ferdi-
nand Reus), National Geographic Creative (BEVERLY
JOUBERT, Cyril Ruoso/Minden Pictures), Shutterstock
(imagIN.gr photography, Sergey Uryadnikov)

Library of Congress Cataloging-in-Publication Data
Riggs, Kate.
Hippopotamuses / Kate Riggs.
p. cm. — (Amazing animals)
Summary: A basic exploration of the appearance,
behavior, and habitat of hippopotamuses, the large
African mammals. Also included is a story from folk-
lore explaining why hippos live mostly in water.
Includes bibliographical references and index.
ISBN 978-1-60818-612-9 (hardcover)
ISBN 978-1-62832-218-7 (pbk)
ISBN 978-1-56660-659-2 (eBook)
1. Hippopotamus—Juvenile literature. I. Title. II.
Series: Amazing animals.
QL737.U57R54 2016
599.63'5—dc23   2014048708

CCSS: RI.1.1, 2, 4, 5, 6, 7; RI.2.2, 5, 6, 7, 10;
RI.3.1, 5, 7, 8; RF.1.1, 3, 4; RF.2.3, 4

First Edition HC 9 8 7 6 5 4 3 2 1
First Edition PBK 9 8 7 6 5 4 3 2 1

AMAZING ANIMALS
HIPPOPOTAMUSES

BY KATE RIGGS

CREATIVE EDUCATION • CREATIVE PAPERBACKS

The hippopotamus is an animal related to whales. Its name means "river horse." There are two kinds of hippos. Both are found in or near lakes and rivers in Africa.

A hippo keeps its head above the water to breathe

Everything about a hippo is big. Its body is shaped like a giant barrel. Its four legs are thick. A human child could stand inside a hippo's open mouth.

A hippo's teeth can be up to 20 inches (50.8 cm) long

Male common hippos can weigh up to 8,000 pounds (3,629 kg). Most female common hippos are about 3,000 pounds (1,361 kg) lighter. The pygmy (*PIG-mee*) hippo is much smaller. It weighs less than 600 pounds (272 kg).

Pygmy hippos enjoy muddy riverbanks and forest swamps

Birds help hippos stay clean by picking bugs off their skin

Like other **mammals**, hippos have hair. But it is not thick. A hippo's eyes, ears, and nose are on top of its head. It keeps most of its body underwater to stay cool.

mammals animals that have hair or fur and feed their babies with milk

Hippos leave the water at night. They look for food. They like to eat grasses and other plants. Sometimes they eat fruit that falls to the ground.

A hippo eats about 88 pounds (40 kg) of food every night

A pygmy hippo stays with its mother for up to three years

A hippo **cow** has one **calf** at a time. A mother hippo helps her young move around in the water. Sometimes she lets her calf ride on her back. Hippo calves drink milk from their mothers. They play with other calves.

calf a baby hippo

cow a female hippo

Pygmy hippos live in pairs or alone. Other hippos live in groups called pods. One male takes charge of a pod. He fights other males that try to move into the pod. Hippos can live for 50 years in the wild.

Fighting hippos throw water and use their heads and teeth

A hippo opens its mouth wide to warn others to stay away

Adult hippos keep calves safe from **predators**. Lions and hyenas try to take calves. Sometimes crocodiles attack, too. Hippos roar to scare away predators.

predators animals that kill and eat other animals

Wild hippos can be scary. But hippos in zoos and parks are safe to watch. They are also safe from people. It can be fun to watch these big animals poke their heads above the water!

Adult hippos can hold their breath for about five minutes

A *Hippo Story*

Why do hippos live mostly in water? People in Africa told a story about this. Long ago, hippos lived on land. They ate everything in sight but were never full. The other animals wanted the hippos to leave land. But they did not want them to eat all the fish, too! The hippos broke their teeth and promised to eat plants. And hippos have been in the water ever since.

Read More

Claybourne, Anna. *Hippo*. New York: Bloomsbury, 2012.

Hatkoff, Isabella, Craig Hatkoff, and Paula Kahumbu. *Owen & Mzee: The True Story of a Remarkable Friendship*. New York: Scholastic, 2006.

Websites

Owen & Mzee
http://www.owenandmzee.com/omweb/
Learn more about a real hippo named Owen and his tortoise friend Mzee.

San Diego Zoo Kids: Hippopotamus
http://kids.sandiegozoo.org/animals/mammals/hippopotamus
Watch a baby hippo and learn more about these animals.

Note: Every effort has been made to ensure that the websites listed above are suitable for children, that they have educational value, and that they contain no inappropriate material. However, because of the nature of the Internet, it is impossible to guarantee that these sites will remain active indefinitely or that their contents will not be altered.

Index